CHOOSING
ME

CHOOSING ME

Love Letters from a Poet

BILL WEBER

Copyrighted Material

Choosing Me: Love Letters From A Poet
Copyright © 2016 by Bill Weber.
All Rights Reserved.
No part of this publication may be reproduced, stored
in a retrieval system or transmitted, in any form or by any
means - electronic, mechanical, photocopying, recording or
otherwise - without prior written permission from
the publisher, except for the inclusion of brief
quotations in a review.

For information about this title or to order other books
and/or electronic media, contact the publisher:
Quality Choices
2607 Zent Drive
Vandalia, Illinois 62471
www.BillWeberAuthor.com

ISBNs:
Hardcover: 978-0-9971317-0-3
Softcover: 978-0-9971317-3-4
eBook: 978-0-9971317-4-1

Printed in the United States of America
Cover and Interior design: 1106 Design

To my wife, my partner, my lover, and my best friend,
Cynthia S. Becker. She is the inspiration for my
creativity and the woman of my dreams.

And she is the one who insisted that the world will be
a much better place when more people can think,
feel and say these things to each other.

Cynthia is the one who encouraged me to publish
these poems for the world to read. And so if any of
the words of this book touch your life,
Cynthia is the one to thank.

Contents

Introduction		ix
How To Read This Book		xv
1	Holding Hands	3
	Every Woman's Body	4
	Vulnerable	7
2	Lips Dancing	10
	Every Woman	13
	Never Ending	15
3	If I Had The Chance	19
	Women And Trees	20
	Feminine Fingers	22
4	With You	27
	Made To Be Touched	29
	Sweet Caress	31

5	Magnetized	34
	Radiance	37
	Warm Sun	39
6	Move Slowly	42
	You Are Every Woman	45
	Lily Petals	46
7	Loosening Buttons	51
	Soft	53
	Heaven On Earth	54
8	Your Lips	59
	Touching You	61
	Fountains Of Heaven	63
9	Choosing Me	67
	Your Sacred Flower	68
	Within	71

Acknowledgments	73
Contributing Photographers	75
About The Author	79
Other Publications By Bill Weber	81

Introduction

Please Read

Making love is so much more than physical pleasure. The intensity of the experience rescues us from the voice in our head and anchors us in our body. It erases the mental distractions of the past and future. It wakes us up into the present moment, in our body, where life unfolds. It dissolves the illusion of separateness and gives us a taste of what it is like to realize our oneness.

Sexual experience is craved for these reasons, and for these reasons it is intensely sacred. It's meant to be a joyful and fun celebration, revered and respected as a sacred practice. And it should be practiced and enjoyed as often as possible.

Choosing Me

How This Book Came To Be

When two people first fall in love, the passion of romance and physical attraction occupies a very large portion of their mental space. They are attentive, romantic, affectionate, seductive, and responsive to each other. It's spectacularly healthy, fun, and enlivening.

I have always wondered how it is that so many people allow that passion to fade. It is a fundamental part of our nature. Why not keep it alive?

I never intended to write poetry. However, I knew that words were powerful and I knew that when I managed to say the right words, in the right way, at the right time, it could be profoundly meaningful for other people.

When it came to romance, like most guys, I had no clue what to say or when to say it. If I happened to come up with the right thing at the right time it was a lucky accident. Some of us fumble along and gradually get a little better through trial and error. But keep in mind that when men are experiencing feelings for their lover, the language center of the brain is not the area being enriched with an oxygenated blood flow.

Introduction

I never thought of myself as a poet. I only wanted to really, really, understand how I experienced my lover's body so I could describe it to her in ways that made sense to her. I wanted her to understand how deeply important her lovemaking was to me. I wanted to know what made sense to her so I could give that to her.

For many years I wanted to describe for her the depth and intensity of my experience of making love with her, but the words were never adequate. I wanted to go beyond all the usual cliché and explanations. For every layer of my experience that I managed to describe, I always discovered an even deeper experience than the words expressed.

I asked myself for the right words. I asked the universe for ways to communicate my experiences that really spoke to her. As I struggled, day after day, to find more meaningful words to describe the depths of what making love with her meant to me, the experience of making love also grew deeper and richer. The more I sought to understand and describe the experience to her, the more intensely sensuous it became.

As the intensity and the pleasures grew, I realized that something magical was happening. An incredible gift was awakening from deep inside us. Making love was becoming for us a sacred practice, a sacred practice into the Devine order of the universe. The more we recognized the sacredness of our bodies and the sacredness of the experience, the deeper, richer and more fulfilling the physical pleasures became.

Gradually, deeper descriptions and more meaningful words came into my mind. And the words turned themselves into verses. And the verses became poems. Poem after poem wrote themselves in my mind. They often wrote themselves much faster than I could write them down. Many came and went before they could be captured on paper.

There is a collective spiritual awakening taking place on our planet right now. I believe that these poems came through the collective unconscious of all mankind as a part of human awakening. They came because I asked for them. They came because I kept asking until the floodgates opened. I was given so much more than I could have ever expected. These poems are here to help you awaken if you are willing. They are here to help all of us awaken to our true spiritual nature.

Introduction

I hope that they touch your life deeply. I hope you enjoy them intensely and share them often. Share them with all of humanity.

Choosing Me

How To Read This Book

Go slow
Read one or two each night
Let your lover know
As you turn down the light

Go very slow
Hold someone close
And never let them go
Enjoy every little dose

Go very very slow
Kiss and touch
Let sensations grow
Give and receive much

Go very very very slow
Experience each word
Enjoy your lover's glow
Show your lover what you heard

Part 1

Holding Hands
Every Woman's Body
Vulnerable

Choosing Me

Holding Hands

When your hand touches mine
Energy melts together
Racing thoughts slow down
Breathing smooths and deepens
Encompassing full body sigh of relief

Femininity in your touch softens the edges
    of maleness
Softness of sweet energy fills in the gaps
Attention comes back into the here and now
The oneness of our beingness envelops
Balance is restored

Choosing Me

EVERY WOMAN'S BODY

A woman's body is a precious gift
A magnificent masterpiece of living art

A woman's body is to be admired and respected
Every part more breathtaking than the next

A woman's body can never be ignored
Irresistibly captivating all attention

A woman's body is made of love
Glowing aura of feminine compassion

A woman's body is alive and responsive
Intricate interactive world of perfection

A woman's body beckons to be loved
Feminine passion waiting to be released

A woman's body is made to be gently caressed
Every part slowly and tenderly enjoyed

A woman's body is made to be cherished
Every curve and shape enjoyed and kissed

A woman's body is made for enjoyment
Stimulating excitement with every taste

A woman's body is heaven on earth
You are my heaven on earth

Choosing Me

VULNERABLE

    Sweetness of your attention
    Warmth of your heart
    Release of my fears

    Joy of your femininity
    Smoothness of your lips
    Vulnerableness of my surrender

    Exhilaration of your sensations
    Overwhelmingness of your love
    Fulfillment of my dreams

Part 2

Lips Dancing
Every Woman
Never Ending

Choosing Me

LIPS DANCING

Your lips are the curves of voluptuous figure
Long and smooth from beginning without end
An hourglass of femininity

Perfect balance of soft and fullness
Moist and inviting
Deliciousness of sweet dessert

And then they move
Gracefully sleek
Rhythmically balanced

All words fade into background
Coherency tries to focus
But I can no longer speak

Each movement absorbing more attention
Heart pounding, blood flowing
Trying to resist the urge to touch

Dancing erotically before my eyes
My lips quiver with need to connect
Feeling all of me in your caress

Fantasies of being loved by you
Feeling your kiss on my skin
Sensations of your lips loving me

Words are but sounds in the background
Vision melted with sensations of you
Heart is yours for the taking

Choosing Me

Every Woman

Every woman is beautiful at every age
As a woman matures her beauty evolves
The essence of her femininity grows in clarity
    with time
Her attractiveness expands to include much more
    than girlish eye appeal

Her presence more disarming
Her lips more compelling
Her kiss more intoxicating
Her touch more stimulating than ever

The depth and power of her femininity evolves
A much deeper attractiveness radiates around her
A richer feminine energy that engages all
    of the chakras
The ageless timeless beauty of femininity
    becomes her

Choosing Me

Never Ending

Kissing you slowly
Touching you slowly
Loving you very slowly

Pausing with every breath
Pausing for every sensation
Pausing to enjoy every inch of your sweetness

Tasting your textures
Feeling your responses
Enjoying the wonders of your body

Experiencing your femininity
Experiencing your responses
Experiencing each wave of pleasure with you

Never ending kiss of love
Never ending kiss of pleasure
Never ending pleasure of kissing the body
    of an angel

Part 3

If I Had The Chance
Women And Trees
Feminine Fingers

Choosing Me

If I Had The Chance

If I had the chance
To gaze into the depth of your eyes
To touch the softness of your hair
To say the words you long to hear

If I had the chance
To hold your face in the palm of my hand
To open the radiance of your truest beauty
To be everything you long to have

If I had the chance
To kiss your lips with the warmth you deserve
To caress your skin like the precious treasure
   that you are
To fill every need before you ask

Choosing Me

WOMEN AND TREES

They come in all shapes and sizes
With various colors, textures and patterns
Each one a unique masterpiece of God's artistry

Breathtaking beauty in full bloom
Turns a man's head and stops him in his tracks
Grabs a man's attention and takes away
    his words

Steadiness grounded deep within the earth
The comfort of shade and shelter from rain
Colorful songbirds singing sweetly

Gentle whisper of soft breezes through the leaves
A solid trusted place to lean
An oasis of comfort and retreat

Multiple layers of pleasure awaits
The fortunate man taken into her arms
The delicate touch of such feminine leaves

The personalness of her sweet caress
Her knowingness of what you need
Her willingness to please

Choosing Me

FEMININE FINGERS

And then you reach for me
Feminine fingers finding my skin
Goose bumps spiraling up my spine
Heart racing, blood surging

The woman I crave is wanting me
Her feminine fingers searching for me
Like the fingers of an angel choosing me
Sensations of heaven enveloping me

Anticipating waves of pleasure
Your sweet caress approaching
Anticipation overwhelming
Hoping, praying, needing you to take me there

And then you find me
Electric explosion of sensuous love
Mind is gone, body is yours
Pure sensations of your sweet femininity

Two bodies becoming one
Two minds realizing oneness
Oneness of being demonstrated in ecstasy
The depth of the universe in the hands
    of my angel

Part 4

With You
Made To Be Touched
Sweet Caress

Choosing Me

With You

Every night with you is a gift
Every touch more exciting
Every kiss gets sweeter
Every sensation even better

Every morning with you is a gem
Every hug more comforting
Every snuggle gets sweeter
Every caress even better

Every moment with you is a treasure
Every hour more fun
Every day gets sweeter
Every year even better

Choosing Me

Made To Be Touched

A woman's body is made to be touched
Soft sensual pleasure of smoothness
Endless curves designed to be followed
Stimulating textures beckoning love
Encouraging responses with each caress
Angelic being in sensual body

Choosing Me

SWEET CARESS

Yearning to be fully loved right now
Dreaming of being wanted in this way
Hoping for your feminine advance
Feeling the exhilaration of your touch

Starting to feel accepted by you
Becoming safer to let myself go to you fully
Losing myself to your caress
Releasing completely to you

Completely vulnerable to your feminine advance
Time stands still in your love
Your energy envelops us
A universe in each sensation

All of my body in your caress
All of my being in your love
All of me in your hands
All of my consciousness in your heart

Part 5

Magnetized
Radiance
Warm Sun

Choosing Me

MAGNETIZED

Masculine eyes magnetized by your sweet
 femininity
Those most beautiful expressions of your
 womanhood hold me captive
The right amount exposed and the rest imagined

I am powerless before their magical beauty
    and presence
Just being in the same room with you disarms
    my self-control
Knees weaken, heart pounds and blood surges

Imagining sensations of your smoothness
    against my face
Tasting beautiful textures of your precious peaks
    in my mind
Hoping you desire my lips to love you here

Dreams of experiencing your attention override
    all thoughts
Embarrassed by my inability to hide such desire
Sweet femininity fulfill the longing
    of my manhood

Choosing Me

Radiance

A woman's body is a spiritual expression of love
A depth of radiance that intoxicates
    consciousness
Erasing the illusions of time and space
Compelling the unity of yin and yang
Expanding our beingness beyond the limits
    of mind
Spiritual ecstasy through sensual connection

Choosing Me

Warm Sun

Warm sun on my back
Gentle sounds of feminine pleasure
Smoothness of your thighs against my cheeks

Intoxicating aroma of feminine arousal
Exploring every layer, every fold
Being encouraged by every response

Sacred nectar of loving passion
Stretching ever deeper for every drop
Encouraging every drop with silky smooth caress

Feeling like a man
In ways words can never describe
Invited into the center of all

Part 6

Move Slowly
You Are Every Woman
Lily Petals

Choosing Me

MOVE SLOWLY

move slowly
touch
love
take your time

feel fully
caress
receive
kiss the skin

breathe with
enjoy
let go
lose conscious thought

be present
relax
melt
roll with waves

merge bodies
drift
be
feel energy rise

Choosing Me

YOU ARE EVERY WOMAN

Being with you is like being with
Every woman I have ever been with
Every alluring woman in every movie
Every beautiful woman in every magazine
Every woman I have ever been attracted to
You are the culmination of all my desires
You are every woman I have ever dreamed of
All wrapped up in one

Choosing Me

LILY PETALS

Your inner thighs like the petals of a newly opened lily
Long, smooth and sensually captivating
Drawing me into the center of the flower

Drawing me into the intricate textures of this most
    sacred place
The place from which new life is born into the world
Lush and hypnotic garden of pleasure and passion

Intricate variations of textures and taste
Your most private and sacred place for me
Deep down between the petals that unfold

Revealing your secret and breathtaking beauty
Allowing me to taste your sweet nectar
To give me the gift of your feminine nature

Fulfilling my manhood with this sacred kiss
My lips, my tongue to the core of your being
Craving every nuance, every curve, every drop

Wanting to be totally immersed in your femininity
Wanting to wrap my lips around all of you
And love every inch of the sweetness of your being

Wanting to swallow all of you and hold you in
    my heart
And love your body to the peak of ecstasy
I love you beyond the depths of consciousness

Part 7

Loosening Buttons
Soft
Heaven On Earth

Choosing Me

Loosening Buttons

Loosening buttons with fingers
Unhooking binding around you
Releasing your treasure from heaven before me
Inviting the sweetness of love's caress

Sliding my cheeks along feminine curves
Tasting your skin with my lips
Hearing your heart beating in my ear
Losing myself in the sweetness of sensations

Kissing in circles around angelic softness
Spiraling slowly toward each peak
Rising and falling with each breath
Breathing in tandem as one

Absorbing of yang into fullness of yin
Melting of two hearts into one
Fading of Illusion into reality of oneness
Dissolving of time into ecstasy of presence in you

Choosing Me

Soft

Soft and smooth like a fresh cool pillow
Alive and vibrant with ageless femininity
Gentle cool energy absorbing me into yourself

Hearing the rhythm of your heart beating
Expansion and contraction of your chest
    breathing
Soft moans of feminine pleasure from an angel's
    voice

Totally here, totally vulnerable, totally yours
Immersed within your feminine sensuality
Two bodies, One being, I am yours

Choosing Me

HEAVEN ON EARTH

Solitude of the trees through the windows
Rhythmic breathing of an angel in my arms
Comfort of your head against my chest

Stroking your hair with my fingers
Kissing the top of your head
Aliveness of our bodies breathing together

Tight clothing released by an angel's hand
My body being gifted with the most feminine
 of all gifts
Myself being chosen by this angel's love

Smooth caress of angelic lips
Heavenly textures of an angel's tongue
Sensations beyond this earthly plane

All muscles relax into your feminine softness
Illusions of time and space are gone
Masculine form becomes one with feminine
 energy

Totally filled with the sweetness of your love
Totally succumbed to angelic femininity
Totally vulnerable to your will

Femininely coaxing my very essence to you
Overwhelming joy of being so wanted
Ingesting the depths of me into the depths
 of your heart

Part 8

Your Lips
Touching You
Fountains Of Heaven

Choosing Me

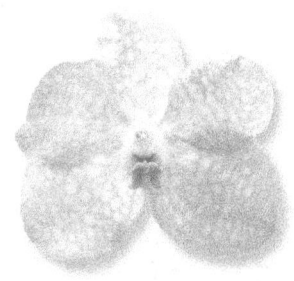

Your Lips

Even as you talk, your lips hold my attention
In my imagination I feel their softness against me
I imagine the gentle pull and release on my skin
From each imagined kiss
Genuine tingles down my spine at the mere
    thought you

Captive to the innocently seductive movements
    as you speak
Trying to catch my breath
Trying to recover
Trying to stay conscious of the conversation
But with little success

Fighting the urge of my lips to join yours
Holding myself back for fear of rejection
Hoping that you would just take me over
Dreaming that you would place your lips on mine
And we would then melt into oneness together

Choosing Me

Touching You

Every part of your body fascinates me
Each movement draws me in
Every inch begs me to touch

To slide my hands over every curve
To explore the beauty of every bend
To enjoy the sensuousness of every shape

Every inch more feminine
Each part more compelling
Every shape a sensuous delight

To receive the purity of heaven distilled
    into physical form
To taste the sweetness of femininity breathed
    into life
To experience the incarnation of an angel
    before me

Choosing Me

Fountains Of Heaven

Warm smoothness
Soft caress
Sweet gentle sensations

Skin meeting skin
Lips kissing lips
Soft breasts against my chest

My heart beating in yours
All of me deep within you
Your femininity fulfilling my being

Hearts beating in tandem
Auras glowing as one
Souls remembering their origins

Waves of ecstasy rising
Fountains of heaven flowing
Energy of creation releasing

Part 9

Choosing Me
Your Sacred Flower
Within

Choosing Me

CHOOSING ME

Am I being wanted in this way
Am I being accepted at this level

Could someone really want me this much
Could someone actually accept me in this way

Am I being chosen to be loved in the most
 personal way
Am I being gifted with the most intimately
 feminine love

Could the woman I want most want to love me
 so personally
Could the woman of my dreams really want me
 this way

Choosing Me

YOUR SACRED FLOWER

The most beautiful place in the universe
Your secret flower
Like the petals of a sacred rose
Blossoming before my eyes

Each petal surrounded by and folding
    into the next
Each layer more fascinating than the next
Each fold more succulent and inviting
Each movement surrounding and calling me

Into the moist center of life within
So sweet, soft and receptive
Ready to receive my kiss of love
Ready to give back its warm silky elixir
    for the soul

Rewarding every kiss with sensual intoxication
Every moist caress balancing my manliness
Melting all my senses into your body responding
Into the limitlessness of your femininity

Illusion of separation and time dissolves
Becoming pure experience of oneness
Realizing our oneness together is ecstasy
You are my reward

Choosing Me

WITHIN

Time standing still
Eternalness of blissful surrender
Energy of femininity taming the driving force
    of masculinity
Essence of masculine form releasing to the gentle
    coaxing of feminine love

Receptivity of femininity loving the essence
    of masculine form
Masculinity feeling his essence lovingly consumed
    within her feminine form
Sacredness of complete and unconditional giving/
    receiving
Yin reaching into Yang releasing Yang into Yin

His physical essence glowing within her heart
Illusion of separateness melted away
Beauty of oneness fills the mind
Love's fulfillment as one

Acknowledgments

Special Advisor, Consultant and Coach:
Cynthia S. Becker

Editorial and Technical Support:
Marcia and Terry Fieland

Additional Advise and Support:
Hurd & Associates Design

Contributing Photographers

The following photographers generously donated their photos and courageously agreed to allow me to alter, modify, Photoshop and overlay their photos in any way I chose to create these and future beautiful presentations for you.

Jack Nichols: Photographer, Jack Nichols

Christine Wuertz: Photographer, Christine Wuertz® is a photographer/graphic designer from the St. Louis, Missouri area. She works as a designer and screen printer.

Eileen Witte: Photographer, Eileen Witte, is someone who is very drawn to flowers and on occasion sees something, a flower, a grouping of flowers, a magnificent sunset, a butterfly, an abstract, that she wants to keep, so she takes a picture of it, and like all things she puts her heart into they turn out amazing.

Carol Madding: Photographer, Carol Madding, resides in Mariposa, California, on the border of the Sierra National Forest, and creates beautiful photographs of all kinds that capture the beauty and emotional character of her subject matter. Having fun with her photos, she has created wonderful memory books for young children. In addition to photography she is an accomplished actor in movies and commercials, published singer, writer, and grandmother.

Carmel Beth Kemmerling: Photographer, was born and raised in Southern Connecticut and ventured to the Midwest to attend Tarkio College, receiving a BA in Biology/Psychology. She fell in love with the midwestern atmosphere and small town charm and continues to reside there. She works as a Business Office Manager at a Long Term Facility in NW Missouri. In her free

Contributing Photographers

time enjoys her artistry capturing flowers, scenery and people through the eye of her camera.

Gibb: Photographer, Gibb, lives in Colorado and enjoys gardening and cooking for friends.

Tiger Lily Flower Shop: A special thanks to all the women at Tiger Lily in Vandalia, Illinois for so generously allowing me to take pictures of their outstandingly beautiful flowers.

About The Author

Bill is a devilishly handsome hopeless romantic living a charmed life. Bill and his radiantly beautiful princess goddess soul mate, Cynthia Becker, live in an enchanted castle on top of a hill on the outskirts of the legendary city of Vandalia, Illinois. Bill's life is like a magical fairy tale where dreams come true every night, and oftentimes during the day as well.

OTHER PUBLICATIONS BY BILL WEBER

Get Sleep Healing, by Bill Weber and Cynthia S. Becker (Audio Recording)

www.ingramcontent.com/pod-product-compliance
Lightning Source LLC
Chambersburg PA
CBHW050441010526
44118CB00013B/1628